Ramadan Recipes

From Our Holiday Table to Yours

Samantha Sanchez

ONE UMMAH PUBLISHING

ISBN 978-1-7321644-0-6

Library of Congress Control Number 2018940563

Printed and bound in the United States of America

First printing April 2018

Publishers:

One Ummah Publishing

oneummahbooks@gmail.com

http://www.oneummahpublishing.com

Millstone Township, NJ

609-831-2181

Dedication

By the grace of Allah

To my family who inspires me to cook with love and

for all their support

To my friends who shared their homes and traditions

Table of Contents

Introduction

The recipes herein are a celebration of the foods served at the most festive and spiritual time for Muslims around the world. I have included recipes that I make traditionally during this time of year. In addition, I have added recipes that have been enjoyed in the homes of friends who invited us for iftar. Lastly, I have included recipes that our American Muslim family enjoys and that have become part of *our* traditions.

It is my sincere hope that you will enjoy cooking and baking things you may not have tried before. The spirit of Ramadan is about community. Breaking fast with friends and family or at the community masjid, we share our traditions and flavors as well as our love and care for each other.

Ramadan evokes different memories in different cultures. The sound of the drummer, the lights, the lanterns. Here in the United States, new traditions have become the fabric of Ramadan. Companies like Modern Eid, Silver Envelope, Eidway and others, have created innovative and beautiful ways for us to adorn our homes and tables.

Although the focus is not on the food during this month, it is in the shared experience of fasting and feasting that we are reminded of all the blessings we have. The recipes were chosen because they exemplify the blessed season in some predominantly Muslim cultures, often evoking childhood memories. Some foods are prominent because they are mentioned in the Quran and sunnah, such as dates, olives, pomegranates, etc. But most of all, they were chosen keeping in mind that you don't have to stay in the kitchen all day long. Simple, easy recipes that are still traditional comfort foods. Ramadan reminds us that we are one ummah and in selecting foods from across cultures, we are able to experience the holy month in a most beautiful way.

Prophet Muhammad(peace and blessings be upon him) said:

"Eat together and mention the name of Allah (God)over your food. It will be blessed for you."

[Abu Dawud]

Ful Medames

No Bake Energy Bites

Suhur Satisfiers

Suhur is the pre-dawn meal. It is usually eaten as close to the adhan time as possible. Heavy foods are normally avoided as are especially salty foods. All around the world, people enjoy both savory and sweet dishes for suhur. In some countries a drummer roams the neighborhood waking everyone up to share in this meal. Proteins and carbs are important components of this morning fare. Along with water, most people enjoy tea or coffee.

Ful Medames

This is an Egyptian staple, sold from carts as street food. I can fondly remember seeing the large metal jug called a qidra and the comforting smell wafting through the air. Young or old, rich or poor, ful is a staple. It is prepared at home in a variety of ways. Our family enjoys this as a suhur meal that sustains you for the whole day.

prep time
5 min

cook time
15 min

serves
4

things you need

15 oz can
Ful (fava beans)

1/2
Onion, chopped

1 tsp
Unsalted butter

2 tbsp
Cilantro, chopped

1 tsp
Chili powder

8 oz can
Tomato sauce

1 tsp
Minced garlic

1 tsp
cumin

1 tsp
Coriander

1 tbsp
Lemon juice

directions

1   In a medium pot, add the butter and sauté the onion.

2   Add the ful and sauté for one minute. Using a wooden spoon, gently mash the beans.

3   Add the remainder of ingredients except for the lemon juice and simmer for 15 minutes.

4   Garnish with a sprig of cilantro.

5   Add the lemon juice and serve.

helpful notes

Serve with pita bread and boiled eggs.

You can put this in your Instant Pot on the slow cooker setting or in your slow cooker on low for 6-8 hours, as traditionally, it is cooked overnight in the large metal jug.

Feta Spread

This spread/dip is widely enjoyed throughout the Middle East and Turkey. It has several variations, some which include green pepper or herbs. The briny goodness of the feta combined with the perky vegetables make this a dip that will keep you coming back for more. The zero cooking time makes this a suhur favorite!

prep time
5 min

cook time
none

serves
4-6

things you need

8 oz
Bulgarian feta cheese

2
Plum tomatoes, chopped

1
Cucumber, finely chopped

2 tbsp
Plain Greek style yogurt

1 tsp
Olive oil

directions

1   Place the cheese in a mixing bowl and mash with a fork.

2   Add the yogurt, tomatoes and cucumber. Mix well.

3   Garnish with oil before serving.

helpful notes

Serve with warm pita bread for dipping. Additional yogurt can be added if you like a more creamy consistency.

Fresh, minced parsley or mint can be added.

Palacinke

A friend of mine from Montenegro once showed me how to whip up these palacinke (pah-lah-CHEEN-kah). These crepes can be enjoyed as a dessert as well. These days, young American Muslims and their families have been seeking out 24 hour restaurants and diners for a stack of pancakes or other breakfast treats for suhur. Here is a nod to a classic recipe and to new traditions.

prep time
5 min

cook time
15 min

serves
4

things you need

1 cup
All purpose flour

1 1/4 cups
Whole or 2% milk

2
eggs

Cooking spray or butter

Fillings:

Nutella
Strawberries
Blueberries
Bananas
Chocolate creme
Jam
Kaymak (Turkish clotted cream)

Toppings:
Chocolate syrup
Maple syrup
Powdered sugar
Honey

directions

1   Place the ingredients in a mixing bowl and beat with an electric mixer.

2   Spray a 10 inch nonstick skillet with cooking spray or grease with butter.

3   Spread 1/3 cup of the batter in the pan. Swirl around the batter in the pan to coat the bottom.

4   Cook until lightly brown on the first side, then flip. Once cooked, gently remove from the pan. Repeat with the rest of the batter.

helpful notes

To serve, choose any fillings or toppings you like. I have suggested some here, but the sky's the limit. Place a spoonful inside the crepe and roll it closed.

Shakshouka

Shakshouka means "shake". Its origin is debatable as Egyptians, Tunisians and others have claimed it as their own. The fact remains, this one pan wonder will please your palate and ward off hunger. A win-win!

prep time
10 min

cook time
20 min

serves
4-6

things you need

1
Green pepper, finely chopped

1
Onion, finely chopped

1 tsp
olive oil

2 cloves
Minced garlic

1 tsp
cumin

1 tsp each
black pepper and salt

1 tsp
Coriander

8 oz can
Tomato sauce

1 tsp
harissa (optional)

4
Eggs

2 tbsp
parsley, chopped

directions

1   In a cast iron skillet, add the olive oil, garlic, onion, and pepper. Season with salt, black pepper, cumin and coriander.

2   Cook on medium heat, stirring occasionally until the vegetables soften.

3   Add the tomato sauce and harissa and cook for about 10 minutes more.

4   Crack the eggs over the tomato sauce in a fried egg style and cook for about 5 minutes or until the eggs are to your desired doneness.

5   Sprinkle the parsley on top before serving.

helpful notes

Harissa is a Moroccan hot chili pepper paste.

If you don't have harissa, use sriracha, or a tsp of chili powder, or omit entirely. Serve with pita or crusty bread.

You can serve with feta cheese on top as a garnish as well.

No Bake Energy Bites

A riff on Oatmeal Raisin Cookie balls and Angel Kisses, two American classic no bake "cookies". These bites combine the best of both while using dates for a Ramadan perfect, nutrient packed punch. Protein galore! Adapted from *Minimalist Baker*.

prep time
5 min

cook time
none

serves
6-8

things you need

1 cup
Old fashioned oats

1 cup
Dates, pitted

1 tsp
cinnamon

1/2 cup
Smooth peanut butter or other nut butter

1 tbsp
honey

1 tbsp
Ground flaxseed

1 tbsp
Chia seeds

2/3 cup
Coconut flakes

directions

1   Mix all of the ingredients except the coconut in a food processor until well blended.

2   Use your hands and get a bit messy! Pinch off a small amount, approximately a teaspoon in size, and roll into a ball.

3   Continue with the rest of the mixture. Makes about 25-30 balls. Roll balls into the coconut to coat.

4   Refrigerate for 1 hour before serving.

helpful notes

They can be stored in the refrigerator for about a week or in the freezer for a longer time.

This is a great use of excess dates during Ramadan!

Instead of peanut butter, you can use almond or cashew butter or use your food processor to process nuts you already have on hand. If you have nut allergies, alternatives based from soy or sunflower seeds work well.

Zucchini Omelette

In Egypt, this is called eggah. In Lebanon, ejjah. Persians call it kuku. The baked version reminds me of the Spanish tortilla. In our house, omelettes are a favorite and we like them any way we can get them, no matter what you call them!

prep time
5 min

cook time
5 min

serves
2-4

things you need

4
Small zucchini, cut in 1/2 inch slices

4
Eggs, beaten

1 tbsp
Onion, finely chopped

2 tbsp
Butter, unsalted

Salt and pepper to taste

directions

1 In a small frying pan, fry the onion and zucchini in butter until tender.

2 Season the eggs and pour over the zucchini.

3 Cook over low heat without stirring.

4 Serve hot.

helpful notes

This can be baked instead of using the stove top. Bake at 300 F until eggs are cooked through. Tomatoes or eggplant can be used instead of zucchini. Feta cheese can be added as a garnish as well as parsley.

Easy Rice Kheer

Traditionally, rice kheer is a labor of love, as cooks can spend anywhere from 1-3 hours making this delectable pudding . This version is great for Ramadan as you can set it in your slow cooker or Instant Pot the night before to serve for suhur, or in the morning to be ready by iftar time as a dessert. Instead of standing over your stove, set this up and get back to your Quran reading. You're welcome! Adapted from *Feed Your Temptations*.

prep time
5 min

cook time
8 hours on low

serves
6

things you need

4 cups
Whole milk

1/4 cup
basmati rice

1 can (14 oz)
Sweet condensed milk

1 tsp
Ground cardamom

1 tsp
Rose water

For garnish
Slivered, blanched almonds, or chopped pistachios, and golden raisins, and saffron

directions

1   Wash the rice three times to remove starch. Drain.

2   Put the milk, condensed milk, rice, and cardamom in the slow cooker.

3   Set the slow cooker on low for 8 hours, or place in the Instant Pot on Slow Cooker setting.

4   When done, mash the rice a bit with a fork, and add the rose water.

5   Allow to cool, then refrigerate for several hours. Add the garnish before serving.

helpful notes

This can be served as a dessert as well.
It can be served chilled or at room temperature. Chilling the kheer will allow it to thicken more, if you prefer a thicker consistency.

Empanadas

Fattoush

Iftar Starters

After a full day of fasting, sometimes up to 16 hours long with no food or drink, one has to "open" the fast or break it slowly. In some homes, this means having a small snack before praying maghrib and then continuing onto dinner. In other homes, it is like an appetizer that directly precedes the main meal. From soups and salads, to fried, savory treats, these iftar starters will be a satisfying way to begin your meal.

Harira

In Morocco and Algeria, it isn't Ramadan without a bowl of harira at iftar time. This "starter" is so filling it could stand alone. This hearty meat and legumes stew will warm your belly after a full day of fasting.

prep time
5 min

cook time
35 min

serves
6

things you need

6 cups
water

1/4 cup
lentils

2 tbsp
rice

3 tbsp
Flour in 1/4 cup of cold water, mix to make paste

2
Medium onions, chopped

1 clove
Garlic, minced

1/2 lb
beef or lamb in 1/2 inch cubes

2 tsp
Olive oil

1 tsp
Butter

2 tbsp
Ground coriander

1/8 tsp
Saffron

15 oz.
Chick peas, drained

1/2 cup
Chopped parsley

8 oz can
Tomato sauce

Juice of 1 lemon

Salt and pepper to taste

directions

1   In a large pot, bring the water to a boil and add the lentils and rice. Simmer for 20 minutes.

2   Add the flour and water paste to thicken, stirring frequently. Set aside.

3   In a frying pan, brown the meat and onions in the oil and butter. Add the garlic and spices and enough water to cover. Simmer until the meat is tender.

4   Add the meat mixture to the lentils and rice. Add the chick peas, tomato sauce, and parsley.

5   Simmer for 15 minutes. Add the lemon juice and serve.

helpful notes

Alternatively, you can serve with lemon wedges instead of adding the lemon juice.

Boiled eggs sprinkled with salt and cumin can be served alongside to make this even more hearty.

Some versions feature broken pieces of vermicelli or spaghetti. You can add that at the end and simmer for an additional 5-7 minutes.

Uzbek Potato Salad

In my dear Uzbek friend's home I enjoyed this Uzbek take on the Russian Olivje (Olivier) Salad. Olivier Salad was created by Lucien Olivier in the 1860s. It spread throughout Eastern Europe and Central Asia. The Uzbek version uses beef or lamb. Though I have eaten my fair share of potato salad over the years, the addition of beef is quite interesting and delicious.

prep time
10 min

cook time
25 min

serves
6

things you need

3
Medium potatoes, peeled

3
Large eggs

1
Carrot, peeled

1/2 lb
Cubes of boiled beef

2 tbsp
mayonnaise

4 oz
Canned Green peas, drained

3
Kosher dill pickles

Salt and pepper to taste

Dill for garnish

directions

1   In a large pot, boil the potatoes, carrot and eggs, until the vegetables are just tender.

2   Allow to cool, then dice the potatoes and carrot. Peel the shell off of the eggs and dice.

3   Dice the boiled meat and pickles. Place all the ingredients into a bowl. Add the peas and mayo and mix well.

4   Season with salt and pepper, and garnish with dill.

5   Chill for 1 hour and serve.

helpful notes

If you will not serve immediately, you can dice and refrigerate the ingredients without adding the mayo until ready to serve.

Alternatively, you can use leftover roasted meat such as beef or lamb.

For a non-meaty twist, you can substitute a can of tuna or crabmeat.

Pakora

Enter a Pakistani home for iftar and you will be greeted by the smell of freshly fried morsels known as pakora. These come in a wide variety, but the vegetable ones are our favorite. These are the tempura of the Desi world. Any other vegetables can be substituted.

prep time
10 min

cook time
5 min, or
until golden

serves
8

things you need

2 cups
Chick pea flour

1 tsp each
Garam masala and curry powder

1/2 tsp
Crushed red pepper flakes

1 tsp
Baking powder

1 tbsp
cilantro, chopped

Salt to taste

1 cup
Frozen cauliflower, cooked and chopped

1
potato, peeled and grated

1/3 cup
Canned green peas, drained

1
Onion, finely diced

approximately 1 cup
Water

Canola or corn oil for frying

directions

1   Mix the flour, spices, cilantro, and baking powder in a bowl. Add about a cup of water or enough to make a thick batter.

2   Add the vegetables and coat well with the batter.

3   Heat the oil in a frying pan and drop spoonfuls of the mixture into oil.

4   Fry until golden and drain excess oil on a paper towel lined plate.

helpful notes

Chick pea flour can be found at an Indian grocery or online.

For a lighter version, spoon the mixture onto a baking sheet lined with parchment paper and bake at 450 F for 10 minutes on each side, or until golden. Serve with your favorite chutney.

Other vegetables to use instead of the potato are: cauliflower, cabbage, peppers, or eggplant. You can also use a combination of these.

Fruit Chaat

If you have never tasted fruit chaat you are in for a treat. I was pleasantly surprised that these spices combined with fresh fruit are refreshing and yummy! The dish is also versatile, allowing you to change the fruits according to the season or make it creamy to satisfy your sweet tooth.

prep time
20 min

cook time
none

serves
8

things you need

1
Mango, chopped

2
Apples, chopped

2
bananas, sliced

2 cups
Seedless Black grapes

1 cup
Pomegranate seeds

1 cup
papaya, chopped

2
Tangerines, sectioned

2 tbsp
sugar

1 tsp
Chaat masala

1/4 cup
Orange juice

directions

1 In a large bowl, toss together all of fruits.

2 Make a dressing using orange juice, sugar and chaat masala. Pour over the fruits and mix well.

3 Cover with plastic wrap and chill for 2-3 hours.

helpful notes

For an added benefit, add 1 tsp of chia seeds to the dressing. Mix well.

Fruit chaat masala is available pre-packaged in most halal or Asian groceries.

To make your own chaat masala:

1/4 cup coriander seeds, 1 tsp cumin seeds, 1 tsp carom seeds. Dry roast in a pan one spice at a time. Allow to cool and grind in a spice mill. You can also use a mortar and pestle. Then, add 1 tsp of dried mango powder (amchur), 1 tsp ground black pepper, 1 tsp salt, and 1 tsp ground ginger. Store in an airtight container.

You can use different fruits according to the season or your taste.

To make a creamy version, use half the orange juice. Fold in 1 cup of whipped cream.

Fattoush

A well known Middle Eastern mezze, the colorful vegetables and the vibrant dressing, accompanied by the crunch of the pita, elevate this salad to the next level. Add grilled chicken and make it a light meal.

prep time
10 min

cook time
10 min or until golden

serves
6-8

things you need

2
Pita breads, cut in bite sized pieces

2 large
Cucumbers, chopped

2 large
Tomatoes, chopped

1/2 cup
Flat leaf parsley, chopped

1/2 cup
mint, chopped

1 large head
Romaine lettuce, chopped

1
Onion, chopped

1/2 cup
Lemon juice

1/4 cup
Olive oil

1 tsp
Salt

2
Cloves of garlic, minced

1 tsp
Ground sumac

directions

1   In a large bowl, toss the vegetables and herbs.

2   In a separate container, make a dressing using the lemon juice, oil, salt, garlic and sumac. Mix well and set aside.

3   Brush the pita pieces with olive oil and toast under the broiler until golden.

4   Just before serving, add the pita and dressing.

helpful notes

The pita pieces can be fried instead of toasted.
Crumbled feta cheese can be added to salad.

Shourbat Ads (Lentil Soup)

This lentil soup warms the soul. Nutritious, delicious, savory...it has just the right blend. My friend's mother taught me how to make this. I watched, taking notes, but her method used no measurements as you can imagine. This is my version of her wonderful and simple recipe.

prep time
5 min

cook time
60 min

serves
4-6

things you need

7 cups
Chicken stock

2 cups
Dry red lentils

2
Tomatoes, peeled

4
Garlic cloves, chopped

1 tsp
Chili powder

3
Onions, peeled

2 tbsp
Butter, unsalted

2 tsp
cumin

1 tsp
salt

1 tsp
Black pepper

directions

1   In a large saucepan, bring the stock to a boil. Add the lentils, tomatoes, and garlic.

2   Quarter 2 of the onions and add to the stock. Chop the remaining onion and set aside.

3   Cover the pot and simmer for 45 minutes or until the lentils are tender.

4   In a small skillet, melt 1 tbsp butter and sauté chopped onion until browned.

5   Allow to cool for 10 minutes. Then, using an immersion blender, puree the lentil mix gently, leaving a slight texture. Season and stir in the remaining butter. Reheat.

6   Before serving, sprinkle the sautéed onions on top.

7   Serve with lemon wedges.

helpful notes

If you do not have an immersion blender, allow the soup to cool completely and pour half of it into a regular blender. Pulse slowly, then return to the pot to reheat. This will retain some texture. If you prefer it smooth, you can puree it in its entirety.

Bolani

This recipe doesn't use the traditional flatbread dough, but the results are excellent. Quick and easy to make right before iftar, as they are best served hot. Thanks to my dear Afghani friend for teaching me this recipe one evening while invited to her home. The best invites are those where you can pull up your sleeves and help with the preparation, sharing the workload and the blessings.

prep time
5 min

cook time
10 min

serves
5

things you need

10
Egg roll wrappers

2
Potatoes, peeled

1
onion, finely chopped

1 tsp
Salt

Water in a bowl for dipping fingers

Oil for frying

directions

1   Boil the potatoes until soft and able to be mashed.

2   Mix the onions into the mashed potatoes adding a few tbsp of water while mixing.

3   On a flat surface, take one egg roll wrapper and fill it with a heaping tbsp of the potato mixture. Using the back of the spoon, spread it out on the wrapper.

4   Dip your finger in the bowl of water and using your finger, wet the edges of the wrapper. This will help the wrapper to seal.

5   Take the end and fold it like a triangle, pressing it down on the edges to ensure sealing.

6   Repeat with the remainder of the wrappers. Fry until golden.

helpful notes

An alternative filling is to use the green part of 2 bunches of chopped leeks.

This can be served with coriander chutney or yogurt, though they are absolutely scrumptious alone.

Empanadas

Most of the homes I have had the pleasure of visiting have served some form of samosas or sambusak, tasty fritters with different fillings and levels of spice. In our home, our Latino heritage provides the perfect fritter. This picadillo is my mother's recipe. As the smell of the picadillo rises, the empanadas will barely reach the plate before being whisked out of the kitchen.

prep time
15 min

cook time
20 min

serves
10

things you need

Picadillo:

2 lbs
Ground beef
1
onion, finely chopped

1 tbsp
cumin
1 each
Green, yellow, and red peppers, finely chopped
2
Roma tomatoes, finely chopped
1/2 jar
recaito

2 tbsp
Golden raisins
10
Manzanilla olives with pimiento, chopped

Salt and pepper to taste

Dough*:
10
Dough circles or Discos, defrosted

Oil for frying

Flour for preparing empanadas

directions

1   To prepare the picadillo, brown the meat and spices in a skillet. Pour off the excess fat and set aside. In a separate pan, add the onions and peppers and fry in 2 tbsp of oil until soft.

2   To the onions and peppers, add the raisins, tomatoes, recaito and olives. Let this cook for about 5 minutes. Then, add the meat to this mixture.

3   On a flat and lightly floured surface, take one dough circle and fill it with a heaping tbsp of the picadillo mixture.

4   Fold into a half moon to enclose the filling. Pinch the edges together into little pleats. Alternatively, you can use the tines of a fork to press the edges together.

5   Repeat with the remainder of dough circles.

6   Fry until golden and drain on a paper towel lined plate.

helpful notes

Some alternative fillings to use are: cheese, chicken, shrimp, or crab.

*A time saving tip is to use this prepared dough known as discos which can be found in the freezer section of your supermarket or online. Recaito can be found in a jar in the Spanish food section/aisle of your supermarket.

For a lighter version, you can brush these with an egg wash (1 beaten egg and 1 tbsp milk) and bake on a greased cookie sheet at 375 F for 15 minutes or until golden.

Stuffed Grape Leaves

Chicken Tagine

The Main Event

Iftar is the meal eaten at sunset. We anxiously await the adhan or call to prayer that lets us know it is time to eat. These meals can be on a larger scale if you have invited guests over for dinner. Or they can be simple with just your family. Any of the recipes will translate well to feed a crowd by increasing the portions.

Oven Baked Scalloped Potatoes (Saniyet Batates)

A wonderful dish to serve for guests as the layered potatoes make a delicious display. Egyptians love vegetables in sauce and this is no exception. The combination of flavors here is spot on!

prep time
15 min

cook time
60 min, or until tender

serves
8

things you need

6
Potatoes, peeled and sliced into 1/4" pieces

3
Roma tomatoes, sliced

8 oz can
Tomato sauce

2 cups
Chicken broth

1 tsp
Garlic powder

2
Onions, chopped

1 tsp
cumin

1 tsp
Paprika

1/4 tsp
Ground cardamom

Salt and pepper to taste

Olive oil to coat pan

Chopped parsley or cilantro for garnish

directions

1 Preheat oven to 350 F. Prepare a large baking sheet or pizza pan and coat the bottom of the pan with olive oil.

2 Layer the potatoes, tomatoes and onions into pan.

3 Mix the tomato sauce, chicken broth and spices, and pour over the vegetables.

4 Bake for about 1 hour or until the potatoes are tender.

5 Garnish just before serving.

helpful notes

You can add sliced zucchini or carrots to this to bulk it up even more.

Chicken Tagine

A Moroccan tagine or stew is traditionally made in a clay pot. However, you can still create great flavor without this pot by simmering the stew in your slow cooker or Instant Pot.

prep time
30 min

cook time
6 hours

serves
8

things you need

1
Onion, chopped

3
Cloves garlic, minced

1/2 cup
Dried apricots and/or prunes, chopped

2 cups
Chicken broth

1 cup
Baby carrots

1 tsp
Cinnamon

Olive oil to brown chicken

8
Chicken legs and thighs

1 tsp
cumin

1 tsp
ginger

1 tsp
tumeric

1 tsp
Chili powder

Salt and pepper to taste

Juice of 1 lemon

Green olives for garnish

directions

1   In a skillet, sauté the onion and set aside. Next, brown the chicken pieces. Then, place the onions and chicken in the slow cooker. Alternatively, use the sauté option on the Instant Pot.

2   Add all other ingredients and mix well.

3   Cook on low (or using Instant Pot on slow cooker setting) for 6 hours.

4   Garnish with olives before serving.

helpful notes

Dates or other dried fruits can be substituted according to your taste and what you have on hand.

Make this into a Persian khoresh! Omit the olives and substitute advieh mix for the spices. To make advieh, combine 1 tsp each of cinnamon, cardamom, coriander, turmeric, and a 1/2 tsp of cumin and nutmeg. If available, add 1 tsp of ground rose petals. (Adapted from *My Persian Kitchen*)

Uzbek Lamb Palov

I first enjoyed this dish in my friend's home. Though she made it sound like it was easy peasy (as all excellent hosts do!), her method seemed a little labor intensive. They say good things come to those who wait. But I wondered how I might be able to get similar results in a shorter time. I used her ingredients and the Instant Pot method which I adapted from *Silk Road Chef*.

prep time
30 min

cook time
35 min

serves
8

things you need

2
Large onions, sliced

1
Head of garlic, unpeeled

4 cups
Long grain rice or Basmati

6 cups
Chicken broth

3
Carrots, peeled and shredded or julienned

Lamb fat or olive oil for browning

2 lb
Lamb, cubed

2 tbsp
cumin

1/2 tsp
Saffron or turmeric for color

2 tbsp
Ground coriander

1 tsp
paprika

Salt and pepper to taste

directions

1   Wash the rice 3 times. Drain well and set aside.

2   On the sauté setting, brown the lamb fat, carrots and onions. If you do not have lamb fat, use olive oil. Add the cubed lamb and brown that as well.

3   Then, add the broth and spices and set on the stew setting for 15 minutes.

4   Let it sit for 10 minutes then release the pressure. Add the rinsed rice to the top without mixing. Add the unpeeled head of garlic to the middle of rice.

5   Set on pressure cook for 10 minutes then release pressure. Remove the garlic head. Fluff with a fork.

helpful notes

Traditionally, this is cooked in a *kazan* or cast iron pot. So if you don't have an Instant Pot, use the traditional method. In a large pot, sauté the meat, carrots and onions as above, simmering the meat until tender, then adding the rice and spices cooking until all liquid is absorbed. You will need an additional cup of broth using this method.

Want to use up leftover roast lamb? Trim the fat for use in sautéing and cube the meat. In step 3, only stew for 10 minutes. Proceed with the rest of the recipe as above.

Moroccan Lamb Chops and Couscous

I love couscous! The first time I had real Moroccan style couscous was on a very large platter with mounds of couscous followed by a generous pile of delicious vegetables and topped with chunks of lamb. To cut time, I provide a recipe here that uses lamb chops as they can be grilled in a much shorter time. This is, by no means, an authentic preparation of couscous but the results are similarly delicious.

prep time
30 min

cook time
30 min

serves
6

things you need

12
Lamb rib chops

1 cup
baby carrots

15 oz can
Chick peas

1 cup
butternut squash, peeled and cubed

1 cup
Zucchini, chopped

2 cups
Couscous

4 cups
Chicken broth

2 tbsp
Golden raisins

8 oz can
Tomato sauce

1/2 tsp
cinnamon

1 tsp each
Cumin and ginger

Juice of 1 lemon

Olive oil

Ras el Hanout to rub on lamb chops

Salt and pepper to taste

directions

1   Rub lemon juice, olive oil, salt, pepper and ras el hanout spice on the lamb chops. Refrigerate overnight.

2   Before grilling, take out the lamb chops and allow them to come to room temperature.

3   Preheat the grill or broiler. Meanwhile, in a pot, place all the vegetables, raisins, tomato sauce, cumin, cinnamon, ginger, and 2 cups of chicken broth.

4   Stew the vegetable mixture until soft. In another pot, bring the remainder of the chicken broth to a boil.

5   Turn off the heat and put couscous in the pot of broth. Keep covered for 5 minutes then fluff with a fork.

6   Grill the lamb chops on high heat for 3 minutes per side. Then lower heat to medium and cook for another 5 minutes. Allow them to rest before serving. To serve, place a portion of couscous on the plate. Spoon the vegetable stew on top of the couscous and finish with two lamb chops on top.

helpful notes

Substitute garam masala for ras el hanout or equal parts of cumin, coriander, ginger, and cinnamon, and ground clove.

Turkish Rice Pilaf

What is better than a perfectly molded, fluffy rice pilaf?! Not much! The buttery flavor is amazing. A simple dish that can accompany almost anything. This is my children's favorite style of rice.

prep time
5 min

cook time
25 min

serves
8

things you need

2 cups
Long grain white rice

1/4 cup
orzo

1 tbsp
Butter, unsalted

3 1/2 cups
Chicken broth

Salt and pepper to taste

directions

1   Rinse the rice in a strainer under cold water and set aside. In a pot, melt the butter and add the orzo. Stir continuously over medium heat until light brown.

2   Add the rice and stir making sure the butter has coated all the rice.

3   Add the broth, salt and pepper and bring to a boil.

4   Cover and reduce to low heat. Simmer about 15 minutes or until all the liquid is gone and the rice is tender.

helpful notes

Use a small dessert bowl as a mold to shape the pilaf for plating. Fill the bowl, packing it down with the back of a spoon, then invert.

Broken vermicelli can be used instead of orzo.

Rinsing the rice gives a fluffier result.

Beef and Okra Stew

Bamieh bil lahmeh or okra and meat stew is comfort food. The key to cooking this dish is using the baby okra also known as okra zero. This dish is healthy and hearty making it a perfect, one pot iftar meal.

prep time
5 min

cook time
70 min

serves
4-6

things you need

1
Onion, chopped

3
Cloves garlic, minced

1/2 bunch
Cilantro, minced

2 cups
Chicken stock

14 oz package
Frozen okra zero

2 lbs
Beef for stew, cubed

1 tsp
cumin

1 tsp
coriander

8 oz can
Tomato sauce

1 tsp
Chili powder (optional)

Salt and pepper to taste

Canola or olive oil for sautéing

directions

1   Preheat the pan with oil. Lightly sauté the okra, then set aside. Brown the beef cubes. Add the onion and cook until translucent. Add the garlic and cook for an additional minute.

2   Then, add the spices and stock. Cover and simmer for about 45 minutes or until the beef is tender.

3   Next, add the okra and tomato sauce, and simmer for an additional 25 minutes.

4   Okra should be tender. Add lemon juice before serving.

5   Serve with rice or pita bread.

helpful notes

Omit the beef and serve as a side dish or use lamb cubes instead of beef. The addition of a 1/2 tsp of cinnamon will give this recipe a more Yemeni flavor.

Lightly frying the okra keeps it from becoming slimy in texture while stewing.

Okra zero can be found in most halal or Middle Eastern groceries. If you cannot find this, use regular sized okra, taking precautions not to overcook or the result will be quite slimy in texture.

Filo Meat Pie (Goulash)

I never understood why Egyptians call this goulash. I guess being American I will always confuse that word for the Hungarian stew. In Greece, this is called kreatopita. Literally, meat pie. Our favorite version is lamb. Layers of yum!

prep time
30 min

cook time
45-60 min

serves
12

things you need

1
Onion, minced

1 package
Filo dough, thawed in package

1
Egg, beaten

1 cup
Whole or 2% milk

1 lb
Ground beef or lamb

1 tsp
cumin

1 tsp
allspice

1 tsp
Chili powder (optional)

Salt and pepper to taste

Olive oil or melted, unsalted butter for brushing filo

directions

1 Preheat the oven to 350 F. Brown the beef or lamb and onions. Add the spices. Then, let cool.

2 Take half the package of filo dough and brush each layer with olive oil or melted butter, layering one sheet at a time in greased 13 x 9 pan.

3 Add the meat mixture on top of the filo sheets. Then, take the remainder of filo and continue the layering process as above.

4 Brush the top generously with oil or butter. With a sharp knife, cut into 12 squares.

5 Mix the egg and milk and pour over the top of the meat pie.

6 Bake for 45– 60 minutes or until golden brown.

helpful notes

Keep the filo sheets covered by a lightly damp kitchen towel as you are working, to prevent them from drying out or breaking.

Slow Roasted Leg of Lamb with Lemon Potatoes

Nothing is as big as our love of lamb. This recipe is a combination of Somali and Moroccan seasonings for the marinade (adapted from *MySomaliFood.com*), while the potatoes are a nod to our Greek heritage.

prep time
30 min

cook time
4 hrs

serves
8

things you need

1
5-6 lb leg of lamb

3
Cloves garlic, minced, separated

1/2 bunch
Cilantro

1
Onion, quartered

2 tbsp
Olive oil

1 tbsp
Ras el hanout (see page 49)

1
tomato, quartered

6
Potatoes, peeled and washed

Juice of 2 lemons, separated

Salt and pepper to taste

directions

1   Place the cilantro, onion, tomato, 2 cloves of the garlic, spices, olive oil and the juice of 1 lemon into a blender. Mix until combined well.

2   Rub the marinade all over the lamb and season with salt and pepper. Place in the refrigerator for at least 2 hours.

3   Cut the potatoes lengthwise in quarters. In a plastic storage bag, add 1 clove minced garlic, the juice of 1 lemon, salt and pepper and a splash of olive oil.

4   Add the potatoes to the bag and allow to marinate in the refrigerator until the meat is in the last hour of cooking.

5   Take the lamb out of refrigerator and allow the meat to come to room temperature. Preheat oven to 450 F.

6   Coat the bottom of a large roasting pan with olive oil. Roast the lamb for 30 minutes uncovered to give a nice browned coating to the outside of the lamb. Then, lower the heat to 325 F and cover tightly with foil.

7   Bake for 3 1/2 hours. The lamb is ready when it is falling off the bone and tender. In the last hour of cooking, place potatoes in a separate baking pan and roast until tender. Remove the lamb from the oven and allow to rest before carving.

helpful notes

Make the marinade ahead, and marinate the lamb overnight for a more intense flavor.

Stuffed Grape Leaves

This is one of the more labor intensive recipes but it is well worth it. If you are like me, you can make this go quickly and bond with your family by enlisting their help in the rolling process. Warah enab, or grape leaves are served throughout Europe and the Middle East. This recipe is my version of my mother in law's (she usually does not include meat) and it is hands down our favorite!

prep time
30 min

cook time
60 min

serves
8

things you need

1
Onion, minced

3
Cloves garlic, minced

1/2 bunch each
Cilantro, dill, parsley, minced

2
Chicken bouillon cubes, crushed

1 cup
Long grain rice

1 jar
Grape leaves

1 lb
Ground beef or lamb

1 tsp
cumin

1 tsp
coriander

8 oz can
Tomato sauce

1 tsp
Chili powder (optional)

Salt and pepper to taste

directions

1   In a pot, add the meat, onion, garlic, herbs and spices. Cook until the meat is browned.

2   Allow to cool. Then add the rice, crushed bouillon cubes, and tomato sauce. Mix well.

3   Coat the bottom of another pot with olive oil. Rinse the grape leaves in water to remove brine.

4   Take one grape leaf and place shiny side down. Place a spoonful of the meat and rice mixture onto the leaf. Roll, tucking in the sides like an envelope. Squeeze gently. Place in the pot seam side down. Continue with the rest of the mixture and leaves, stacking them as you go.

5   Before cooking, place an inverted plate on top of the rolled leaves to hold them in place. Fill the pot with water up to the plate.

6   Bring to a boil and then simmer for about 1 hour until the rice is tender.

helpful notes

You can prepare the rolls ahead and leave in the refrigerator overnight before cooking. Optionally, you can line the bottom of the pot with meat bones or slices of green pepper before placing rolled leaves in the pot.

Decadent Butter Bars

Sheer Korma

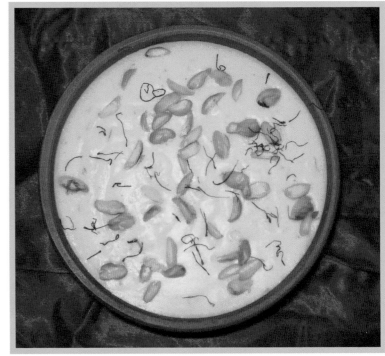

Divine Desserts

A sweet ending to a spiritually invigorating day of fasting. These desserts are simple and yet are well suited for bringing to your host at an iftar. Your family and friends will swoon over this collection of delectable desserts.

Konafeh

This is the Palestinian version of a wonderful dessert served throughout the Middle East. Some versions have custard or cream, but our family prefers the cheese filling. This is akin to the Nablus version without the food coloring. Many thanks to my friend who shared this recipe with me one Ramadan, as it has become a family favorite.

prep time
10 min

cook time
25 min, or until golden

serves
12

things you need

1 package
Kataifi (shredded filo dough)

8 oz package
Shredded akawi or mozzarella cheese

2 sticks
Unsalted butter, melted

15 oz container
Ricotta cheese

1 1/2 cups
Granulated sugar

3/4 cup
water

1 tsp
Vanilla

For garnish
Chopped pistachios

directions

1 In a large bowl, separate and break up the shredded dough. Toss with melted butter.

2 Grease a 9 x 13 baking sheet or pizza style pan, Put half the dough into the bottom of the pan spreading evenly.

3 In a separate bowl, mix the cheeses. Spread the cheeses over dough in the pan.

4 Top with the remaining dough, pressing lightly.

5 Bake at 350 F for 15 min or until lightly brown. During this time, boil the sugar and water for 5 minutes to make a simple syrup. Add vanilla to the syrup.

6 Cut the konafeh into 12 pieces. Pour the hot syrup over the hot konafeh and let stand before serving.

7 Garnish with pistachios.

helpful notes

Serve warm.
Akawi cheese can often be found in Middle Eastern or halal grocery stores. Mozzarella is a great (and economical) alternative.

Maamoul

Beautifully decorated, shortbread style cookies with either a date or nut filling. The crown jewel of Ramadan cookies, these buttery and delicate treats simply melt in your mouth.

prep time
10 min

cook time
25 min, or until golden

serves
12

things you need

Filling:

3 tbsp
Granulated sugar

1 tsp
Orange blossom water

1 tsp
Cinnamon

1 cup
Pitted dates, chopped   _or_

1 cup
chopped walnuts

Dough:

1 cup
clarified butter (samna or ghee)

2 cups
All purpose flour

1 cup
Fine semolina

Pinch of salt

Powdered sugar for dusting

directions

1   Mix the dough ingredients in a bowl.

2   Mix the filling ingredients in a separate bowl. Then, take an amount of dough the size of a walnut and press with your thumb to form a hollow with 1/4" thick sides. Fill with a tbsp of filling, then pinch to close.

3   If the dough is dry, moisten your hands with water while working with dough.

4   Then press the filled dough into the tabi or mold. Gently remove from the mold and place onto a greased cookie sheet. If you don't have a mold, press the cookie down onto a greased cookie sheet to flatten the bottom. Decorate the top using a fork to make lines.

5   Bake at 350 F until lightly golden. Allow to cool, then dust with powdered sugar.

helpful notes

A tabi or mold can be found easily online, either in plastic or wood.
These cookies can be kept in an airtight container for up to one month.

Kazandibi

I am in love with the name of this dessert. It just sounds like fun! It simply means 'bottom of the pot'. This is Turkish burned milk pudding reminiscent of crème brulee. Don't let the name fool you. There is nothing bad about burning your dessert in this recipe! Our family had the pleasure of tasting this amazing dessert on Eid at a local Turkish restaurant and we have been hooked ever since. Adapted from *Turkish Yummies.*

prep time
5 min

cook time
40 min

serves
4-6

things you need

1 tbsp
Unsalted butter for greasing pan

2/3 cup
Rice flour

1/3 cup
cornstarch

4 cups
Whole milk

1 cup
Granulated sugar

1 tsp
Vanilla or rose water

5 tbsp
Powdered sugar

1 tbsp
Cinnamon

Optional:
Chopped Pistachios or garnish

directions

1 Grease a glass 13 x 9 pan and set aside. Preheat the oven to 325 F. Mix the rice flour and cornstarch in a saucepan. Add a little milk, mixing until there are no lumps. Then, add the remainder of the milk.

2 Cook over medium heat stirring constantly for 10 minutes.

3 Then, add the granulated sugar and cook about 3 minutes mixing constantly until the sugar is dissolved and you have achieved a pudding-like texture.

4 Remove from the heat and add the vanilla.

5 Spread a thick layer of powdered sugar onto the greased pan. Place in the oven for 5-10 minutes. The bottom will caramelize. Remove from the oven.

6 Pour the milk mixture slowly on top. Do not disturb the bottom. Bake for 20 minutes. Allow to cool for 1 hour.

7 Then, cool in the refrigerator for several hours or overnight. Flip over onto a platter, garnish with cinnamon and nuts if desired. Cut into squares and serve!

helpful notes

Watch the pan carefully when caramelizing the sugar so as not to burn.

'Ataif

In a tie with maamoul for first place for the most popular Ramadan dessert, 'ataif (or qatayif) is certainly a winner by any standards. Filled with raisins and nuts and dipped into a heavenly sugar syrup, these crunchy treats are a true experience for your tastebuds.

prep time
40 min

cook time
25 min

serves
12

things you need

Pancakes:
2 cups all purpose flour
1 tsp instant dry yeast
3 cups warm water
1 tsp baking powder
1 tbsp sugar

Filling:
1 1/2 cups finely chopped walnuts
2 tbsp golden raisins
2 tbsp shredded coconut
1 tbsp sugar
1 tsp cinnamon

Simple Syrup:
2 cups water
2 cups sugar
1 tbsp of lemon juice
1 tbsp orange blossom or rose water

For garnish
Chopped pistachios

Vegetable or Canola Oil for frying

directions

1   To make the syrup, place sugar and water in a pot and bring to a boil. Boil for 15 minutes. Remove from heat and add lemon juice and orange blossom water. Set aside and allow to cool.

2   To make the batter, mix all the ingredients in a blender then allow it to rest for 30 minutes.

3   Then, heat a greased griddle or frying pan. Once hot, reduce the heat to medium and pour 1/4 cup of the batter for each pancake.

4   Cook only on one side until bubbles appear over the entire surface of the pancake. Carefully remove from the griddle, placing on a cookie sheet and cover with foil to prevent from drying out. Repeat with the remainder of the batter. Allow to cool.

5   Fill each pancake with 1 tbsp of filling. Fold over and press the edges together to seal. Fry until golden.

6   Dip the hot 'ataif into the syrup. Sprinkle with chopped pistachios and serve.

helpful notes

A time saving trick is to purchase ready made pancakes at your local Middle Eastern or halal grocer during the Ramadan season.

You can make the pancakes a few hours ahead and then fill and fry just before iftar. Try different fillings such as Nutella or a mix of different nuts.

Petla

Like a zeppole or a beignet, these Albanian puffs of fried dough are a quick and easy dessert that can be savory or sweet. The Greeks and Egyptians call these loukoumades or luqmat ul 'adi, respectively. A little prep time for the dough leads to a quick and delicious ending to your fast.

prep time
10 min

cook time
5 min, or
until golden

serves
6

things you need

1 cup
Warm water

1 tsp
Active yeast

1 tbsp
Granulated sugar

1
egg

1/2 tsp
vanilla

2 cups
All purpose flour

Pinch of Salt

Vegetable or corn oil for frying

For serving
Powdered sugar or jam and feta cheese

directions

1   Mix the water, sugar and yeast and let stand for 5 minutes.

2   Combine the flour and salt. Add the yeast mixture, vanilla, and egg, slowly mixing until blended.

3   Cover with plastic wrap and let the dough rest for 2 hours.

4   In about 2 inches of hot oil, drop tablespoonfuls of dough moving it around in the oil so it puffs nicely. Turn the balls of dough to be sure both sides cook well.

5   Fry until golden and puffy. Remove with a slotted spoon and drain on paper towels.

6   Repeat with the remainder of the dough.

7   Before serving, sprinkle with powdered sugar or serve with jam and feta cheese.

helpful notes

Use a second spoon to scrape the dough off and into the oil, as the dough is a bit sticky.

An alternative, though nontraditional, way to serve these is to sprinkle with cinnamon and honey or dip in simple syrup.

Sheer Korma

My first Eid was spent with my friend's Indian American family who welcomed me into their home and shared their Eid traditions, one of which is the quintessential Eid dessert of Sheer Korma. Eid is just not complete without it.

prep time
20 min

cook time
20 min

serves
6

things you need

1 cup
Broken vermicelli

4
Cups whole milk

2 tbsp
Unsalted butter

1/2 tsp
Ground cardamom

1/4 cup
Granulated sugar

6 oz
evaporated milk

10
Almonds, blanched and sliced

10
Pistachios, blanched and sliced

5
dates, pitted and cut into 4 pieces

1/8 cup
Golden raisins

1 tsp
Rose water

1/4 tsp
Saffron threads

directions

1   Toast the nuts, dates, raisins and vermicelli in butter and set aside.

2   In a pot, bring the whole milk to a boil then set on low.

3   Add the sugar and cardamom and cook for 5 minutes.

4   Add the evaporated milk, nuts, dates, raisins, and vermicelli. Cook until thickened and the vermicelli is soft (about 10 minutes).

5   Remove from heat and allow to cool for one hour.

6   Add the saffron and rose water and serve at room temperature or chilled.

helpful notes

It will thicken if placed overnight in the refrigerator and can be thinned out a bit with milk.

Decadent Butter Bars

An American Southern classic. These bars are simple and yet result in the most scrumptious dessert you have ever had. Ramadan, for our American Muslim family, wouldn't be complete without these heavenly bites.

prep time
5 min

cook time
30 min, or
until golden

serves
12

things you need

1 box
Yellow cake mix

1
egg

1 stick
Unsalted butter, melted

8 oz
Cream cheese, softened

2 cups
Powdered sugar

2
Eggs, beaten

1 tsp
vanilla

For garnish
Powdered sugar

directions

1   Grease a 9 x 13 pan and preheat the oven to 325 F.

2   In a bowl, mix the cake mix, 1 egg, and melted butter. Press into the bottom of the pan.

3   In another bowl, mix the cream cheese, 2 eggs, vanilla and sugar with an electric mixer on low speed until creamy. Spread over the crumb base in the pan.

4   Bake at 350 F for 30 minutes or until edges are golden brown.

5   Once cooled, place powdered sugar in a strainer and shake over the top. Cut into 12 pieces.

helpful notes

You can serve them plain without the extra sprinkled sugar.
The top layer will be soft but will settle after cooling.
For best cutting results, chill in the refrigerator for 2 hours.

For a Middle Eastern flair, substitute orange blossom water for the vanilla.

Basbusa

Namoura, Revani, by any other name it would be just as sweet. Basbusa is a delectable semolina cake, sweet and moist and soaked in syrupy goodness. It isn't Eid without the sweets, right?

prep time
5 min

cook time
30 min, or until golden

serves
12

things you need

1 1/2 cups
Fine semolina

1/2 cup
Granulated sugar

3 tbsp
Clarified butter (samna or ghee)

6 tbsp
Whole milk

1/2 cup
Shredded coconut

1/4 tsp
Baking powder

1 tbsp
Plain yogurt

For garnish
12 toasted almonds

Prepared syrup from p. 68 using vanilla instead of rosewater or orange blossom water

directions

1   Grease a 9" square pan and preheat the oven to 350 F. Make the syrup and set aside.

2   In a bowl, mix all the ingredients until well blended.

3   Spread evenly in the pan and bake for 15 minutes.

4   Cut into 12—2" squares and decorate with almonds. Return to the oven for 15 minutes or until golden.

5   Remove from the oven. Pour syrup over the cakes immediately.

helpful notes

You can use different nuts as a garnish or omit.

Acknowledgements

If you have not thanked people, you have not thanked Allah (God). This book would be incomplete without acknowledging some very special people which helped it come to fruition.

First, I would like to thank my husband, Hesham, who believed in me when I said I wanted to write a book. Sure, at the time, he had no idea it was a cookbook. Nonetheless, he told me to go for it. His support means the world to me.

To my mother, Marie, who not only nudged me from behind but read every word as my "in house" proofreading editor. Her support is beyond measure. She has always been in my corner helping me follow my dreams.

To my children, Adam, Yasin and Maryam, who cheered me on, enjoyed the taste testing and gave me the bandwidth to complete this. I love you....my biggest fans!

To my friends, who told me I could do it. Thanks for believing in me.

To those who reviewed the book and gave your feedback, your kindness and support will always be remembered.

Index

About the Author

Samantha Sanchez was born and raised in New York. She converted to Islam in 1997 and celebrated her first Ramadan shortly after. Samantha has been (and continues to be) a published poet, cultural anthropologist, school administrator, teacher and author. At the university level, she taught food and culture courses. Her interests in food traditions among cultures of the world is what inspires her. She is a self described foodie. A home cook, with a hearty love of experimentation with different cuisines, she has been collecting recipes from friends and family since she was a young girl, always adding her own twist.

Samantha loves to travel and explore new cultures. She lives with her multicultural family in New Jersey where she cooks with love and plays their family version of "Chopped". She enjoys creating Ramadan and Eid traditions with her family.